KNOW IT NOW!

- SOMETHING DEADLIER THAN NUCLEAR BOMB IS ABOUT TO EXPLODE!
BY
BISHOP OCHEI INNOCENT

Table of Contents

CONTENTS

DEDICATION

To teachers world-wide

PREFACE

I remember my uncle. An ex-soldier and one eyed king in the land of the blind he was a half baked teacher of sorts in the community. Though he went to school, he did not stay long enough to pass the first school living examination. He could hardly spell his own name talk less of being able to read newspapers.

All around him were illiterate. As far as western education was concerned, they only knew where to put the food in their hand!

My uncle fed on exploiting their ignorance. He sold them dummies on many fronts. For instance, whenever they received letters from their sons and daughters in townships, they called my uncle to read the letters to them. He would gladly pretend to read only to use common sense in guessing what the writer wanted to say or was saying and tell it to the people with embellishments.

Unfortunately for him, my grandfather was in phone communication with my immediate father before Dad's letter reached the village. My Dad assured grandpa that the envelop would include a certain sum of money. So when the letter came, my uncle was summoned to read the letter. Unknown to him, grandpa had opened the letter and removed the money. When my uncle "read" the letter, he neither mentioned the enclosure nor what it was meant for. He only said the author sent his greetings and asked for update on the village politics!

Certainly, when people are not educated, they become easy candidates of manipulation and exploitation.

The easier they can be manipulated, the more they can be used as dispensable to the detriment of mankind.

This book takes a look at the consequences of illiteracy in African and Asian countries. It adduces facts to show that the western world cannot be insulated from the negative impacts some which are already being seen in the unmitigated economic migrations plaguing the First World today.

Chapter One

WHAT ARE WE UP AGAINST?

The above question reminds me of the colonial era in Nigeria. Then, it was easier to see a toad jumping about in the afternoon than to see a literate indigene. When the white man came with his education, the wise elders of the land mistook the purveyors as enemies whose wares should not be purchased at all. They did not want to have anything doing with the white man and whatever he stood for. So, many of them shun the idea of western education.

Yet, the colonial masters needed to communicate with the locals in order to bring law and order into the polity. If the people did not understand the administrators or the new laws they were churning out, how would the people obey what they did not understand?

The result was that since the colonial masters could not get the ideal, they settled for less. People with half education like my uncle were adopted as interpreters. These were people who more by omission than commission, were interpreting Queen's English either upsi pockets! Sometimes, when the white colonial magistrate would sentence a guilty but illiterate person to a fine of one goat, the interpreter would ask him for ten goats!

It resulted in a great tragedy! The fact remained that just as the locals did not understand English, the magistrate did not understand indigenous languages! This partly made the people hate the colonial masters whom they saw as high-handed and exploitative whereas the reverse was the case.

Confusion always follows misinterpretation. Wars have even been fought between nations and communities just because their communication was misunderstood by the recipient.

I remember a story. It was told to me by Bishop Noah Adobo who resides in Abuja the beautiful capital city of Nigeria. It is a man who planned to marry into a distant tribe. Normally marriage rites among these people take days, steps and seasons. Since it was far, the intending groom planned to do everything on the same day and take away his bride. So he took his kindred to go and visit the in-laws in good faith. Those that accompanied him had never travelled outside their own tribe. They did not know that when the people they were visiting say" **"Wa"** that meant "come". In their own language, *"Wa"* meant: *"**run away**",* the import being that your life is in danger!" The moment that the visitors heard **"Wa"**, they abandoned all they came with and ran away! Of course, that ended the marriage!

When the current army of illiterates reach out to one another, there will be such disconnect that will pitch the world against each other. Some will run away while others wonder what is happening. History has a way of repeating itself. Is

the past not a picture of what is to
come?

Chapter Two

DO WE HAVE THE WILL TO PUSH EDUCATION?

The importance of education as a whole cannot be over-emphasized. Learned men will gladly tell you that literacy in particular and education as a whole provides the following advantages:

1. It promotes mutual
    understanding between
    persons of diverse
    tongues.
2. It enables the skilled to
    teach the unskilled.
3. It helps preserve
    knowledge from
    generation to generation.
4. It promotes peace since
    people's intentions are
    clearly seen and grasped.
5. It enables the trained
    person to get gainful
    employment.
6. It enables citizens of any
    nation to read and
    comprehend the laws of
    the land and obey them,
    knowing the
    consequences of
    disobedience.

7. It promotes commerce between people of diverse tongues.
8. It helps us to fulfill our dreams by communicating what we want at all times.
9. It promotes health since preventive measures are easily communicated and comprehended by both sides.
10. It saves time since people readily understand one another.
11. It saves cost of looking for and hiring interpreters.
12. It ensures that justice is served through first-hand and proper understanding what the judge feels on the matter.

13. It facilitates international relations since they can understand one another.
14. It reduces incidences of xenophobia.
15. It enables the people to make the right choice at elections since they understand the campaign issues.
16. It reduces racial discrimination because being literate enables us to read literatures on other people's culture and understand their values better.
17. Literacy is a ladder that enables us to climb higher in the society. The more we study, the higher our chance of being hired at top level.

18.   It makes us hungry for more knowledge. The more we know, the more we want to know. Man is curious by nature and that is what fuels research and inventions!

19. It enables us to comprehend news and what is happening in other lands and climes.

20.   It promotes religious harmony as we understand why people of other religions do what they do and to communicate sacraments of our own religion to others without giving them offense. Etc.

Can you imagine a world without literacy and education? Think of man in the Stone Age! Think of when you first visited a country that does not speak your own language! Recall the difficulties you had in buying and selling!

I recall the day I went to Togo for the first time. They speak French while I come from an English speaking country. I wanted to say something as simple as I want to make a phone call but I could not. I got stranded at the park since I could not notify my hosts that I had arrived!

Literacy and education fill a great vacuum! This is how the celebrated author Stephen R. Covey puts it in his best-selling book: *"THE EIGHT HABIT"* *[2004 Edition Page 43.free Press]:*

> ***"The idea of the space between whatever happens to us and our response to it hit me like***

a ton of bricks. Since then I have come to understand that the size of the space is largely determined by the our genetic or biological inheritance and by our upbringing and present circumstances"

Simply put, the author is saying that how we respond to things that happen around us depends on our type of education because education is the value we get from our biological inheritance, upbringing and the things that happen around us to date! In order words, education is so important that it determines how we respond to external and internal stimulus around us! When people are literate and educated, they behave differently from those who are not.

I know that other religious books might have something to say about this topic. I look forward to you telling me what your holy book says but as a Christian, I crave your indulgence to quote the Bible and it says:

"My people perish for lack of knowledge."

[Hosea 4:6]

When people are illiterate, they are not able to widely research and gather information, which when properly applied becomes wisdom and wisdom answers all things! When civilizations lack knowledge, they die. Look for instance, at the people of Nagasaki and Hiroshima in Japan. They perished not because nuclear bombs were dropped on them but because they lacked the know-how as at that time to develop shields against nuclear bombs. Today, many nations have bomb shelters and survive when bombs drop!

Talking about ignorance, consider this too! There is this time worn tale of the ship that was in difficulty at sea. It ran out of drinking water for days. When that need for water was becoming life threatening, the captain sent out mayday SOS messages. As God would have it, a better informed captain received the message. This merciful captain reached out to the stranded one, advising him to lower his bucket and take water from around his ship. The captain in difficulty found it hard to accept. He had been standing on fresh water all this while! He protested but the other one captain insisted that the pained ship was not in any difficulty or danger. It was suffering from the ignorance of its captain and crew. They did not know that they were at the estuary of River Mississippi, the longest river in the world. This long river had the strength and mass to push sea water further away from the shore. By implication, the stranded ship was well within drinkable waters and not surrounded by sea water as the embattled captain and crew had ignorantly thought!

Illiteracy is not just a disease but a fast growing plant and the fertilizer fuel the growth is illiteracy!

In the face of all these, can you this? There are still groups, even in today's world: who consider education an abomination? They are so much against education that they kill to stop children from going to school. They storm schools, armed with machine guns and other repeaters just to hamper education and the benefits that come with it. They gate-crash into schools and kidnap innocent children, take them to the bush and marry them off forcefully! All, just to prevent them from being educated!

It is illiteracy that makes many so ignorant that they keep dumping plastic wastes into sewages and water drains. These drains in turn, empty into the oceans in the long run inevitably killing fish and fauna! Others burn forests and fill our cities with deadly smoke. They are lost as to why the world worries and talk about climate change because of their limited understanding.

 Little wonder that the United Nations has risen to the challenge by celebrating the INTERNATIONAL LITERACY DAY on every 8th of September!

But is this not too little too late?

Chapter Three

CAN THE INTERNATIONAL LITERACY DAY SOLVE THE PROBLEM?

It was enacted on October 26, 1966 by UNESCO General Conference and first celebrated the next year.

The aims of celebrating this day are:

1. To sensitize the world on the benefits of literacy.
2. Highlight the dangers of illiteracy in nations, communities and societies!
3. To set agenda for the world in the fight against illiteracy.
4. It is a day on which attention is drawn to efforts being made by some countries. This will enable others to emulate them.
5. It is also a day to encourage and not condemn those countries, communities and civil societies lagging behind to buckle up!
6. To highlight the connection between illiteracy and severe poverty!
7. To ensure that global efforts on illiteracy agree and align with the UN AGENDA 2030!

United Nations have habitual come up
with celebration goals such as:

1. United Nations Literacy Decade
2. Literacy and Health [2007 -
    2008]
3. Literacy and Empowerment
    [2009-2010]
4. Literacy and Peace [2011-2012]

During these celebrations, summits and
seminars are held by all concerned, to
bring together world leaders and other
stakeholders, including but not limited
to non-governmental organizations and
schools, to brainstorm on the way
forward.

Writers and reporters are also
encouraged to make the need for literacy
an integral part of their plots and
themes!

THE HIDDEN BOMB

The world must not feign notice of the dangers in the exploding numbers! This is dominantly in countries and regions were population growth is based on polygamy. Due to illiteracy, people see family planning and infant disease prevention as poisonous or aimed at ethnic cleansing!

African and Asian countries continue to lead in this alarming direction. According to UNESCO, over 775 million adults world-wide lack literacy. Of these, 60% are said to be out-of-school children while women constitute two-thirds of the figure! Burkina Faso, Mali and Niger rank high in illiteracy and it is noteworthy that violence and insurgency rank equally high in these places. The narrative is that child labor, prostitution and child soldiering are prevalent in these places. People bear children without thought to the future of the kids.

Little wonder that violent groups such as **Boko Haram**, killer Herdsmen, bandits, and coup plotters have found not only safe havens but a fertile recruitment ground for cheap labor in places like that.

Most of the negatives of illiteracy thrive in Afro-Asian such as Bangladesh, Burma, Pakistan, Indonesia, etc. These countries in particular rank among the poorest countries of the world. Surprisingly, Nigeria an oil-producing country is said to be the capital of poverty in the world with about 87 million people living on less than a dollar per day! This makes it easy for hungry mouths to be recruited for the evil that threatens the world today!

The marriage between illiteracy, growing population, dwindling resources, unbridled national borrowing, natural disasters such as desert encroachment and corruption is not a bomb to explode in future. It is already happening. How do you explain the great number of youths and able-bodied men and women who leave these and neighboring countries in droves, risking the high ocean waves, sharks and hazards to cross into Europe?

It is a bomb that if not nibbled in the bud, will be deadlier than nuclear when it climaxes!

Chapter Four

THE WAY OUT

Here is a timely warning:

"Don't short cut the process" says Jeanette Clift George in her book: '*TRAVEL TRIP FROM A RELUCTANT TRAVELLER*" [*Page 22, 1987 Edition. Thomas Nelson Inc.]*. She wisely counsels that anyone who wants a lasting solution to any problem must not short circuit the process! Nothing can be more exact!

The world must go the whole hug. While it is something significant to declare a world literacy day, it is over-riding to:

1. Encourage **free and compulsory education to all levels** in all countries of the world. Countries, particularly Third World nations, should embrace digital and visual education for its many advantages.
2. The world must gear up efforts to curb if not **eradicate corruption**. This canker worm has eaten deep into the financial fabric of emerging nations and must be fought to standstill with no holds barred!
3. **Free and compulsory transfer of skills** and technology to struggling nations.

4. Vigorous and sustained
    **campaign to promote gender
    equality** in all spheres of life.
5. **Debt forgiveness** for heavily
    indebted nations.
6. **Increased** Government and civil
    society **collaborations.**
7. **Development of political will**
    to do the needful among world
    leaders. This should include
    sanctions on those who fail to
    cooperate!

FINAL NOTE

Those who seek to build walls
must know that certain things
cannot be contained by walls of
any kind. When people are hungry
or threatened, they find a way to
survive!

OTHER BOOKS BY BISHOP OCHEI

1. Something Worse Than Witchcraft And Acidic Prayers To Destroy It.
2. Productivity: How to Increase Your Income a Thousand fold!
3. How to Sell the Seemingly Unsellable.
4. Six Things You Must Do Before Age Sixty.
5. Ten Things I like About Africa's Richest Man.
6. How To Increase Your Ministerial Connections
7. The Best Thing You Can Do For Yourself As A Christian

ABOUT THE AUTHOR

Bishop Innocent Ochei is a Research Enthusiast and President of New Dimension Seminaries International.

He is married to Elizabeth, a Pentecostal prophetess and they are blessed with four God-fearing children.

THANK YOU FOR READING

Please if you have any suggestions for the next edition or any other comment, feel free to contact the author on:

newochei@gmail.com

You can also reach him for counseling and prayers.

NOTES

NOTES

www.ingramcontent.com/pod-product-compliance
Lightning Source LLC
Chambersburg PA
CBHW051136250726
48655CB00007B/3097